M000003037

# LINES FOR ALL OCCASIONS

# Breakups & Rejections

KNOCK KNOCK

VENICE, CALIFORNIA

Created and published by
Knock Knock
1633 Electric Avenue
Venice, CA 90291
www.knockknockstuff.com

ISBN: 978-160106056-3
UPC: 825703-50106-3

10 9 8 7 6 5 4 3

# Contents

*"We could give this a few more years, but why?"*

# Introduction

At some moment in every person's
life, it will be necessary to deliver
a breakup or rejection. For most
of us, however, these unpleasant
occurrences arise with reasonable
frequency, whether firing someone,
quitting a job, telling a therapist he
doesn't understand human nature,
delivering news of inadequacy,
turning down a pickup attempt or
breaking up with a lover, or terminating a dysfunctional relationship

with a family member, friend, or pet. The anxiety induced by these situations is among the highest we will face in our jobs and personal lives. Most people lose sleep before dropping the ax, mentally rehearsing how the scene will play out. Those whose fear prevents them from making necessary changes will live diminished lives as they are increasingly surrounded by people who bring them down.

While no guide can alleviate the need to confront an unworkable situation and the person behind it, *Breakups and Rejections for All Occasions* arms you with scripts to end any relationship. Many books address the challenges of being on the other side of the equation—the one who is fired or dumped—but few tackle the equally distressing position of the one doing the dirty work. With *Breakups and Rejections* in your pocket you'll never again be left without the right words.

When choosing your lines, think about your delivery style: Droll? Dry? To the point? Cruel? Also consider your relationship with the about-to-be-terminated. Is it intimate? An acquaintance? Professional or personal? Have they done something truly wrong, such as lie or steal? Next, formulate your desired outcome, both short- and long-term. While it's all-too-tempting to say "Go to hell," such definitive or insulting approaches may come back to haunt you. Life is short and memories are long, so be absolutely certain that the bridge you burn is a bridge you will never again want to cross.

Even when interacting with the worst of rejectees, it's always better to conduct your conversation in person. Modern technology— whether telephone, email, or Post-it—is the coward's way out, and not only will you fail to improve your management of these difficult encounters, you will certainly leave a bad taste in the rejectee's mouth. When the time comes to stage your confrontation, deliver your chosen line with confidence. If you stutter or stammer, hem or haw, the person may not take you seriously. In any rejection or termination situation, you want to achieve an air of courteous, balanced firmness, as well as a somber tone befitting the gravity of the situation. Of course, if your goal is to humiliate, you can also laugh and point.

So many of us have put off difficult encounters. Now, however, you hold in your hands the solution to your problems, your own personal Cyrano de Bergerac. No matter the situation, person, or pet, you'll feel powerful and in control with this panoply of witty, effective lines. And because we all find ourselves on the receiving end of rejection from time to time, you can also work on developing appropriate comebacks should one of these lines be directed at you—after all, there's nothing worse than coming up with things you could have said. Or, you could just pick up a copy of our *Insults and Comebacks for All Occasions*. That's right—here in the Lines for All Occasions kingdom, we've got your back. Don't you feel better already?

9

# YOU'RE FIRED

*When the paycheck will no longer be forthcoming*

FIRING AN EMPLOYEE CAN BE ONE
of the most disagreeable—and
sometimes satisfying—duties an
employer faces, but it's necessary
all too often. One good rule of
thumb for managing personnel is
"Hire slow, fire fast." When it's
time for someone to go, there's
no reason to prolong a mutu-
ally unpleasant experience.

# Tip: When to Fire

Experts disagree on the timing of employee termination. Some say you should fire in the first part of the week so the employee doesn't brood about it over the weekend and so other employees can address their concerns about the firing. Others recommend terminating late on a Friday so the employee can have some privacy and clear the premises discreetly. Ultimately, do it when you feel it's right.

Depending on your working relationship with the employee and the cause of his termination, there are many ways to announce the news. If the employee hasn't stolen or behaved in other unacceptable ways, you can break it to her gently. If your company is a huge multinational with lots of red tape, you'll want to use corporatespeak.

For the lunkheads out there who just might not grasp subtlety, go blunt. Finally, there's always a bad apple who requires the "You're an incompetent freak" approach.

When firing someone, remind yourself that you are doing this for the good of the company and the other employees—not to mention the person being terminated, as no one should stay in a position for which they're not suited or for which the company will no longer pay. Allow any inevitable guilt to be a fleeting moment, and remember that with these lines, you don't even have to think about what you'll say.

# Kinder and Gentler

Let's go talk outside.

———•·•———

We want to wish you luck in
your future endeavors.

———•·•———

Here's your paycheck. You
may notice it's pink.

———•·•———

Think of this as a get-out-
of-jail-free card.

———•·•———

This is as hard for me to say
as it is for you to hear.

———•·•———

Some day soon you may want
to use me as a reference.

———•·•———

These are the days I hate
being a boss, but I won't be
your boss much longer.

I share your pain, though
technically I've never been fired.

———•———

We'll both be happier when you're
free to pursue your other interests.

———•———

Good news! You get to file
for unemployment!

———•———

Here's a box for your
personal belongings.

———•———

You will be missed.

———•———

Don't think of this as a closed door;
look at it as an open window.

———•———

I'd like to take a minute to go
over your severance package.

———•———

Start looking in your
mailbox for your final check.

If you think of "last resort" as a free
vacation, it'll be easier to bear.

———•———

Have you ever heard of COBRA?

———•———

I hope we can still be friends.

———•———

This comes from both the top and the
bottom. The middle had no opinion.

———•———

While you have excellent penmanship
and make great coffee, this company
also values industry-specific skills.

———•———

It's just not working out.

———•———

Don't look at it as losing a job—
think about regaining a life.

———•———

Before I go any further, I'd like to
offer you the opportunity to resign.

## Corporatespeak

We don't look at it as downsizing—
we look at it as *right*sizing.

———•◆•———

Consider this your final job evaluation:
Termination Effective Today.

———•◆•———

You may have noticed we've outsourced
most of our support staff to India.

# Tip: Do It in Person

While it may be tempting to terminate an
employee via remote or electronic means, it's
definitely the cowardly way out and will not
be looked upon kindly. In 2006, RadioShack
was vilified in the press for firing four hundred
workers by email. They dug the hole deeper
by using unclear corporatespeak: "The
workforce reduction notification is currently
in progress. Unfortunately your position is
one that has been eliminated."

17

Management says we have to trim
some fat. You probably already know
that you're tipping the scales.

———•———

There's no room for you on our
new organizational chart.

———•———

Welcome to Outplacement Training.

———•———

I'm sure you've heard the rumors
about the head count readjustment.

———•———

The workforce agreement
is no longer in force.

———•———

The views on your blog are contradictory
to the values of our corporate culture.

———•———

Every failure needs a scapegoat.

———•———

You're being merged out,
effective yesterday.

Redundancies are key to company continuity, but your position is now completely redundant.

<hr>

Headquarters has mandated a paradigm shift, and you're no longer paradigmatic.

<hr>

You've burned your last french fry.

<hr>

You just don't have the adequate bandwidth.

<hr>

Let me reverbiagize: RIF stands for "Reduction in Force."

<hr>

We're delighted to be able to offer you this career change opportunity.

<hr>

Waste expulsion happens.

<hr>

Quite frankly, you're subprime.

# Biting the Mouth that Feeds

Firing doesn't have to be limited to people who work *for* you. Sometimes you have to fire people you work *for*—clients or customers. Take a tip from Sprint Nextel, which in 2007 cancelled the accounts of over a thousand cell-phone customers for calling customer-service lines too frequently. The letter stated, "The number of inquiries you have made to us . . . has led us to determine that we are unable to meet your current wireless needs."

It's simple; you didn't participate in Secret Santa.

———•◦•———

Congratulations! You've been selected to take the payout.

———•◦•———

There's no "i" in "team," and there's no "u" in "employed here."

———•◦•———

Your job is no longer future-proof.

## No Misunderstanding

Hi! I'm your replacement.

---

I'm working on my confrontation
issues—you're fired.

---

I'll make this short—today's
your last day.

---

Your trial period is over.

---

You won't be needing your
office key anymore.

---

I had to make a choice, and I chose you.

---

As this is the night shift, you've
been nocturnally discharged.

---

My therapist says I need to let you go.

I'm so sorry you won't be at the company holiday party this year.

———•———

Since you refuse to quit, I have no choice but to fire you.

———•———

Get the hell out!

———•———

IT will be helping you transfer all your company files to the server before you leave today.

———•———

Take off the chicken suit—for good.

———•———

This is your last chance to take advantage of the employee discount, so you may want to stock up.

———•———

Don't feel bad—this is our fault. We should have never hired you in the first place.

We're moving in a you-free direction.

———•◆•———

I've looked at this from every angle,
and all I can say is, you're acute.

———•◆•———

These security guards are going to
escort you out of the building.

## You're an Incompetent Freak

This isn't business, it's personal.

———•◆•———

We've decided to invest in the
future rather than overcome
the mistakes of the past.

———•◆•———

We've both failed. You failed to succeed,
and I failed to fire you sooner.

———•◆•———

Your performance is not
commensurate with your ego.

Your resumé claimed you were
a self-starter, but the truth is
you're actually a self-ender.

---

We were hoping you'd have
the smarts to catch on.

---

You're not part of the solution,
you're part of the problem.

---

You're in way over your head.

---

Company policy requires
intelligence and good looks.

---

We have a zero-
tolerance policy for morons.

---

We've received one too
many complaints about
your personal hygiene.

You need to look in the mirror.

———•·•———

It has become clear from your
ignorance of basic grammar that you
lied about your college degree.

———•·•———

You've outlived your usefulness.

———•·•———

You take up way too much space.

# Still Royalty-Free

In 2004, Donald Trump attempted to trademark the phrase "You're fired!" (both with
and without the exclamation point), which
he had popularized in his hit television show,
*The Apprentice.* He faced opposition from
a small ceramics store in Illinois that had
previously filed to trademark the phrase as
well as from the makers of the educational
board game "You're Hired!" Trump's applica-
tion was denied.

A team is only as strong as its
weakest player. With you gone
we'll be much stronger.

———•◦•———

Since you have no work ethic, it's
better that you not have any work.

———•◦•———

We've found a machine that
can do your job better.

———•◦•———

The tightness of your
pants has clearly cut off the
blood flow to your brain.

———•◦•———

I'm simply tired of you.

———•◦•———

Your ambition is sorely misplaced.

———•◦•———

I know it'll be hard to tell your
kids that you're an utter failure.

Your personality doesn't serve
you well in the workplace.

———•◆•———

Your oozing acne is a health hazard.

———•◆•———

I know you can't help it, but
others refuse to work with you.

———•◆•———

When we hired you, you were thin.

———•◆•———

We pride ourselves on employing
people with good character.

———•◆•———

You're the lone sadist in a company
culture based on masochism.

———•◆•———

Nobody likes you.

———•◆•———

After I slept with you, I realized
you were expendable.

# I QUIT

*When your career needs a new paradigm*

YOU WOULDN'T BE HUMAN IF YOU weren't just a bit nervous before announcing that you intend to leave a job; it may be one of the most difficult conversations you have with a boss. While you can't prepare for your boss's reaction, you can plan how you present your departure—whether you explain your reasons, express gratitude, recite your list of grievances, or even blow

# Don't Quit—Get Fired!

While it's extremely gratifying to quit your job, it may be more financially beneficial to get yourself fired. Termination without cause will reap you unemployment and, if you play it right, severance pay. Cause-free self-sabotage can be tricky, however, so tread carefully. Start by extending your lunch breaks and getting sick a lot. Escalate to turning in sloppy reports, misunderstanding directions, and moping around.

the whistle. All depends on the professional experience you've had during your tenure and whether you want to maintain or burn a bridge.

In this chapter, you'll find a diverse group of lines for breaking the news. Sometimes it's just time to move on, especially if you're leaving to pursue a life dream. Sadly, you or your company may suffer from an ethics deficit, requiring a different type of approach. Leaving a job is all too commonly motivated by employee underappreciation, in which case it's critical that you let your boss know what you're feeling. Finally, in the worst of circumstances when there's no bridge to be maintained, you'll want to tell your employer that he totally sucks.

When the moment comes that you take a deep breath and walk into your boss's office, remember that she will be stuck there and you get to leave. You are an employee, not an indentured servant—or worse, an owner—who has no choice but to stay. However you choose to express your goodbyes, keep your eye on the prize—you're outta there.

# Moving On

I want to go out while I'm still
at the top of my game.

———•———

This is the best job I've ever had;
I know it'll be downhill from here.

———•———

You will always be the gold
standard of bosses.

———•———

The bad news is that I'm leaving;
the good news is I'm giving
you twelve months' notice.

———•———

I've decided to go back to
school—full-time.

———•———

I believe you deserve someone
who's 100 percent committed.

———•———

I'm pregnant.

I look forward to training
my replacement.

———•••———

It's just not fun anymore.

———•••———

I was meant for bigger things.

———•••———

I always thought I'd be a working
mother, and I appreciate your holding
my job open for me and paying high-
level temps during my six-month
maternity leave, but now that the baby's
here, my priorities have changed.

———•••———

I've learned so much from you that
it's time to start my own business.

———•••———

Though this job has been financially
and emotionally rewarding, I can
no longer deny my dreams.

———•••———

I've decided to be independently wealthy.

I'm disavowing capitalism.

———•———

I've accepted a position that doesn't
require me to wear a uniform.

———•———

I'm moving to an ashram.

———•———

It's my goal to have a dozen
careers by the time I'm fifty.

———•———

I'm dropping out of the rat race.

———•———

I've decided to go freelance.

———•———

I had a vision—it's not this.

———•———

I never meant to stay this
long in the first place.

———•———

If only this job didn't take
all day, I'd stay forever.

I'm losing my identity in
your corporate image.

————•◦•————

I just keep wondering,
"What's it all for?"

————•◦•————

Now that I've slept with
everyone in the department, it's
time for me to move on.

# Mad as Hell

In the 1976 Oscar-winning movie *Network*,
news anchor Howard Beale (Peter Finch) is
going to be fired after his ratings decline.
In response, Beale threatens to commit sui-
cide—on air, live. Allowed back on the show
to apologize, Beale decries the state of the
world and says, "I'm as mad as hell, and I'm not
going to take this anymore!" He asks others
to do the same, starting a national movement
and getting his own show in the process.

# Ethically Challenged

Lying for you was not in
my job description.

---

I'm tired of watching everyone
around here succeed by assmosis.

---

I don't want to go down with this ship.

---

In my professional opinion, this
industry's dead—and you killed it.

---

I haven't forgotten about company
loyalty. I just happen to be more
loyal to another company.

---

Though I've learned some valuable
things about human nature, I want to
leave while I still have some dignity.

---

My whole resumé was a lie.

Please know that I never signed
the confidentiality agreement.

———•••———

If you give me a year's severance pay,
I promise not to testify against you.

———•••———

Before I cleaned out my desk, I called
your wife and told her about our affair.

———•••———

By the time you get this
message, I'll be headed for South
America with the payroll.

———•••———

I'm the corporate leak.

———•••———

After taping together all the
documents you shredded, it's clear
that this isn't the company for me.

———•••———

I did your dirty work to get
ahead, and it got me nothing.

# Tip: To Do Before You Quit

Rather than leaving in haste, plan the steps of your departure. Erase or shred personal information, including emails and anything incriminating. Copy or print out material for your portfolio or future reference (note: this can be illegal). Then, tell your employer. Standard procedure includes writing a resignation letter, giving two weeks' notice, and organizing your workload for the next person. Finally, be sure to get a reference!

The truth is, I quit doing this job six months ago. I've just been showing up to get the check.

---

You've failed to implement one too many OSHA requirements.

---

I refuse to work for a union-busting operation.

You don't recycle.

———•·•———

I don't stand for what you don't stand
for—and you don't stand for anything.

———•·•———

After smuggling office supplies
home over recent months,
I no longer need this job.

———•·•———

It just doesn't seem right that
your office door is locked
so much of the time.

———•·•———

When I was hired, I was told
this was a nonsmoking office.

———•·•———

It's become clear to me that your
ass-grabbing is not accidental.

———•·•———

Too many children have died.

# So Underappreciated

I'm going to miss our Saturday morning
meetings and midnight conference calls.

---

I'm just a number to you.

---

This job isn't exactly the gold
mine you promised.

---

I've got a concussion from
the glass ceiling.

---

While I can honestly say I've learned
a great deal from this experience,
you can pick up your own damn
dry cleaning from now on.

---

I'm too old for this crap.

---

I'm through being blamed
for your mistakes.

You never say "please" or "thank you."

---

The ratio of fulfilling to non-fulfilling is unfavorable.

---

I can't work for a boss who doesn't recognize my genius.

---

I've just made my last pot of coffee.

---

I've just unclogged my last toilet.

---

I have so much more to offer than you're willing to take.

---

My doctor says this job is detrimental to my health.

---

My therapist says I should quit before I kill someone.

I think we can both agree—
everyone hates me.

———•·•———

I'm a creative!

———•·•———

Although it's a thrill to see my ideas
implemented, it's no longer fun
watching you get all the credit.

———•·•———

I'm finally going to take the long
lunch you never permitted—
and I will not return.

———•·•———

Here's my resignation.
Now you can't fire me.

———•·•———

My parents always said I was
special and I could do whatever I
wanted to do, but you don't seem
committed to making that happen.

———•·•———

I'm not your bitch.

## Burning the Bridge

I refuse to continue covering
for your incompetence.

———•◦•———

I was under the mistaken
impression that sleeping with you
would result in a promotion.

———•◦•———

You put the *micro* in *micromanage*.

# The Fake Quit

Richard Nixon had a hate-hate relationship
with the press. In 1960, the media focused on
his unattractive, sweaty look during television
debates with John F. Kennedy, one reason
Nixon lost the presidential election. In 1962,
he ran against another media-popular can-
didate for governor of California, lost again,
and declared, "You won't have Nixon to kick
around anymore, because, gentlemen, this is
my last press conference." Sadly, he lied.

Respect has to be earned.

———•••———

I no longer recognize your authority.

———•••———

I'm through putting up with
your intimidation tactics.

———•••———

You're a Republican—how did you
ever think this would work?

———•••———

You're a total dilettante.

———•••———

I never liked you.

———•••———

I would rather lick dirty
toilets than work for you.

———•••———

I can no longer accept being
publicly berated.

———•••———

You're all talk and no action.

Thanks to you, my self-esteem
has never been lower.

———•———

You can't expect to continually throw
your subordinates under the bus and
have them stay on indefinitely.

———•———

You act like a superstar, but you're not
even a has-been—you're a never-was.

———•———

When I arrive in the morning,
I never know whether to expect
Dr. Jekyll or Mr. Hyde.

———•———

I've incurred hearing loss from
your constant screaming.

———•———

I can't even get my work done thanks to
all your ridiculous rules and regulations
and formatting requirements.

———•———

You're going to hell.

# LETTING GO
# OF THE HELP

*When service providers stop serving*

IN THE TWENTY-FIRST CENTURY, there's no way we can get everything done without hiring individuals to maintain various aspects of our lives. Unlike centuries past when only the rich had help (full-time, of course), now we have diverse part-time independent contractors who make sure the house is clean and the emotions are worked through.

# Tip: Firing Household Help

Be prepared when you terminate someone who's had access to your home, family, and personal secrets. Take an inventory of your belongings, noting whether anything is missing (but do note when it's possible that you or a family member misplaced it—there's no need for dubious accusations). Courteously tell the individual that he or she is no longer needed and discuss the return of any missing items. Finally, change all locks.

This army of helpers makes our lives easier on the one hand, but they also require us to manage mini-empires of personal service. Without management experience, many individuals will find themselves at a loss when the time comes to let someone go, not to mention that these relationships don't follow the standard corporate model and can be very personal in nature. They've been in your house, your hair, and your head. They've cared for your children, your teeth, and your naked body.

Termination approaches will differ depending on the role the person has played in your life. A therapist requires psychological savvy, while a pool cleaner may demand a slightly more blunt delivery. The important thing to remember when you're contemplating the conversation, both before and after, is that you pay this person. If you're not getting the service you deserve, it's best for both of you that you cut ties. After the deed is done, don't look back; instead, focus on finding someone else to meet your needs.

# Therapist

I can analyze my own dreams.

———•·•———

I always leave feeling worse
than when I came in.

———•·•———

The fifty-minute hour is an oxymoron.

———•·•———

You say I need to move away from
denial, and I can no longer deny
that I'm in love with you.

———•·•———

I'm not getting sane fast enough.

———•·•———

We just keep going over and
over the same ground.

———•·•———

Your couch is lumpy.

———•·•———

My obsession with you has cooled.

You've empowered me enough to
say, "I'm never coming back."

―――・•・―――

I've decided to go down
the path of self-help.

## Doctor

You don't validate for parking.

―――・•・―――

I've found another doctor who will
give me pain medication on demand.

―――・•・―――

You think I'm a hypochondriac.

―――・•・―――

It appears that you skipped the bedside-
manner class in medical school.

―――・•・―――

I found a second opinion I liked better.

―――・•・―――

You always insist on weighing me.

# Dentist

I can feel it when you're drilling.

---

I found a dentist who lets me
watch DVDs during treatment.

---

You have such a fetish about flossing.

---

You charge too much for nitrous.

---

I've never seen you wash your hands.

---

I've decided that dentures are my future.

# Housekeeper

You didn't pass the white-glove test.

---

My friends think I'm pretentious
for having a maid.

We're moving to a neighborhood
that's not near any bus lines.

———•••———

I'm having a hard time finding
some of my jewelry.

———•••———

We need someone who can speak English.

———•••———

You're just not skilled enough
at stain removal.

# Channeling Mrs. Beeton

In 1861, Isabella Beeton, Martha Stewart's
Victorian predecessor, published the definitive and charmingly exhaustive Mrs. Beeton's
Book of Household Management. Apply her
terminology as cause for discharging your
household help, including "Sad want of elbow-
grease," "Creaking of shoes an abomination,"
or "Not to . . . offer any opinion, unless asked
for it; nor even to say 'good night' or 'good
morning,' except in reply to that salutation."

You're too chatty.

———•———

You found my secret stash.

———•———

You took my last Vicodin.

## Gardener

I bought my own lawn mower.

———•———

We're putting in a rock garden.

———•———

We're turning our backyard
into a basketball court.

———•———

I've noticed your employees
peeking through my windows.

———•———

Our garden is so overgrown that
our dog got lost for two weeks.

We're spending too much on the housekeeper to afford a gardener.

## Pool Cleaner

I got an acid burn in the Jacuzzi.

———

I can't see the bottom.

———

We're draining the swimming pool for the next few winters.

———

We've purchased a mechanical pool sweeper.

———

This guy came by and said he'd do the same thing for less money.

———

You rebuffed my advances.

———

You don't fill out your Speedo.

# The Majordomo

If you employ a substantial arsenal of domestic help, you should consider hiring someone to do the firing for you: an assistant who can terminate anyone but himself. From *major* (chief) and *domus* (house), a majordomo, common in Europe in the feudal ages, manages your entire estate. He or she speaks on your behalf—including complete management of the other staff. The catch: you may have to hire a new majordomo to fire the old one.

## Hairdresser

You just don't understand my hair.

———•••———

Your personal style doesn't inspire enough confidence for me.

———•••———

I still haven't recovered emotionally from the last haircut.

I don't think my face shape
is suited to the mullet.

———•••———

I'm shaving my head.

## Massage Therapist

I asked for Swedish, you
gave me Shiatsu—in my
book, that's unforgivable.

———•••———

Smooth jazz is for sissies.

———•••———

It turns out I'm ticklish.

———•••———

My doctor told me I'm
incapable of relaxing.

———•••———

I got a massage chair for Christmas.

———•••———

I found a masseuse who's willing
to provide a happy ending.

# Personal Trainer

I just can't work out with someone
who's as fit as you are.

---

My abs aren't responding
the way I'd hoped.

---

You're too critical of my downward dog.

---

Pep is for cheerleaders.

---

If I wanted to be abused, I'd
visit my family more often.

---

I've reached my goal—acceptance
of my body the way it is.

---

I just remembered that vanity is a sin.

---

You make me cry.

## Childcare Provider

The nannycam results are not good.

---

My friend's nanny said she saw you
giving the children non-
organic food at the park.

---

Your bedtime stories are
scaring the children.

---

I don't know where else my toddler
would have learned to swear.

---

The children have started
calling you mommy.

---

My husband mumbles your
name in his sleep.

---

You make the children cry.

## Wedding Planner

I read a book by Martha Stewart
and now feel I can do it myself.

———•———

It's clear that you wish *you* were
the one getting married.

———•———

It doesn't appear that you believe
in our everlasting love.

———•———

We've decided to elope.

———•———

The wedding is off.

## Dog Walker

My neighbor said she saw you
let the dog off the leash.

———•———

My neighbor said she saw you
fail to pick up after my dog.

My neighbor said you spoke
harshly to my dog.

My neighbor said that the dog walks
you more than you walk the dog.

My neighbor said you walk really slowly.

My neighbor said she'd walk the dog.

# Spying on the Nanny

Ever get the feeling you don't trust the nanny?
Most of us are familiar with the notorious
hidden-camera nannycam, but there are other
ways to check up on those caring for your pre-
cious offspring. On nanny-tracking websites
such as ISawYourNanny.blogspot.com, good
Samaritans post sightings of childcare providers engaging in poor behavior. Make sure to
log on with your own sightings to help other
parents such as yourself.

# CRUSHING
# DREAMS

*When their best efforts call for rejection*

WE WOULDN'T CALL THEM DREAMS
if they were easy—getting into
a top-notch college, applying for
that perfect job, auditioning for
a starring role, sending the great
American novel out to publishers,
trying to get a gallery owner to
take on one's art oeuvre, or win-
ning the reality-television lottery.
For those fortunate enough to
crush such dreams, it's important

# Form-Letter Rejection

With the electronic wonders of data merging, a template will allow you to delegate rejection as well as churn letters out by the ream. By keeping the letter general with select fill-in-the-blank areas, a wide range of aspirants can be crushed: "Dear ___: Unfortunately, your ___ does not work for our ___. Good luck with your endeavor." For good authenticity and a personal touch, scan your signature and include it in the file.

to develop a stable of approaches with which to reject supplicants.

Your approach will depend on what you wish to accomplish. Do you want to spare the person's feelings? Do you value honesty such that you'd inform someone that they're barking up an inappropriate tree? Would you prefer an easy way out (lying or euphemizing to some degree), or are you willing to engage? (Follow-up contact is inevitable if you outline specific reasons for rejection and give tips for success.) If someone is bothering you or if their work offends, you may want to be downright cruel. It's all a matter of thinking through your desired impact.

You will no doubt incur some nasty responses from no-talent borderline personalities disgruntled by your rejection. In those moments, just remember that those who haven't yet made it into a position of power don't understand the burden imposed when they ask you to accept or reject them. Until they've reached the top themselves, they never will.

# School Applicants

We get twice as many applications as
slots for new students, and half the
applicants were better qualified than you.

———•—•———

4.0 just isn't good enough for us.

———•—•———

You might want to try
community college first.

———•—•———

There are so many good jobs
available to high school graduates.

———•—•———

We've already filled our quota
for people like you.

———•—•———

Your definition of "extracurricular"
differs somewhat from ours.

———•—•———

As expressed in your college essay,
your life has been too easy.

You can't afford our tuition, but
your parents make too much
to receive financial aid.

————•◆•————

You just seem dumb.

## Job Seekers

Our decision not to hire you
wasn't based on any one thing.

————•◆•————

The virus attached to your
resumé crashed our server.

————•◆•————

Your MySpace page indicates that
you're not ready for a real job.

————•◆•————

Your background check showed
some irregularities.

————•◆•————

Your quoted objective, though
entertaining, reveals a lack of direction.

When you're an hour late for the interview, you can't expect much.

———•—•———

Your salary expectations are completely out of line with your skill set and past experience.

———•—•———

We can't take a chance on a job-hopper.

———•—•———

We'll keep you on file should a future opportunity present itself.

———•—•———

You spent the entire interview bad-mouthing your previous employers.

———•—•———

With all that you have going on, I don't think you could handle this job.

———•—•———

We spell-checked and fact-checked your resumé—clearly, someone had to.

Though your references are glowing, your resumé flawless, and your interview skills exemplary, we've decided to hire someone else.

⸻

You're completely overqualified for the position.

⸻

You just rubbed me the wrong way.

# The Un-Great American Novel

Famed publisher Alfred A. Knopf believed in keeping the door open for future talent. One rejection to an unknown concluded, "One of these days we will have something from you that we can publish with gusto." Knopf was less agreeable with established authors: "Your manuscript is utterly hopeless . . . I never thought the subject worth a damn to begin with and I don't think it's worth a damn now. Lay off, MacDuff."

# Performance Auditions

We're looking for someone with a
more realistic-looking toupee.

———•———

We need someone a little less urban.

———•———

We need someone a little more ethnic.

———•———

We're looking for someone
a little younger.

———•———

We're looking for someone a little older.

———•———

We're looking for someone
a little better looking.

———•———

We're looking for someone
a little more real.

———•———

We need someone who can dance.

We need someone who can sing.

———•◦•———

We need someone who can act.

———•◦•———

You just don't have "it."

———•◦•———

Don't quit your day job.

———•◦•———

Next.

## Literary Submissions

The writing lacks style and the
content lacks interest. However,
the spelling is impeccable.

———•◦•———

Your author photo wouldn't
be marketable.

———•◦•———

I fell asleep by the tenth page.

# The Art of Rejection

Individual reactions to art are notoriously subjective. Whether to declare a work a masterpiece or a piece of garbage can feel completely arbitrary, but with *Contemporary Art Gallery* magazine's list of most frequently cited reasons for gallery rejection, you have plenty to choose from: style, quality, similarity, dissimilarity, low pricing, high pricing, location, logistics and administration, personality clashes, and gallery cliques.

We could reconsider your work at a later date, but it will definitely be an uphill battle.

---

I've read this before—by somebody else.

---

I don't feel anything truly fresh here.

---

I think we can both agree it's not your best work.

We can only publish the
very best submissions.

———•∙•———

Publication of your writing would
do readers a grave disservice.

———•∙•———

You'd be better served by an editor
who's passionate about your work.

———•∙•———

Your autobiography just doesn't ring true.

## Art Portfolios

Your style is derivative and your
framing decisions unfortunate.

———•∙•———

Just because you're self-taught
doesn't mean it's outsider art.

———•∙•———

Your work falls outside the
arbitrary parameters this
gallery has established.

It's not really a stand-alone piece.

———•◦•———

The piece wouldn't fit
through our front door.

———•◦•———

It just doesn't *move* anybody here,
except in the wrong ways.

———•◦•———

You're a premodern artist in
a postmodern world.

———•◦•———

It's not quite gallery-quality.

———•◦•———

The intended dialectic mines the
semiotics of postexpressionistic
symbolism, but it sucks nonetheless.

———•◦•———

A picture may indeed paint a
thousand words, but this
doesn't say anything.

If you are willing to accept my
criticism and start over, I would
be willing to take another look.

————•—————

It's crap. No, really—it's crap.

## Reality Shows

The tribe has spoken. —*Survivor*

————•—————

Please pack your knives
and go. —*Top Chef*

————•—————

Two thumbs down. —*Ebert and Roeper*

————•—————

You are no longer in the
running toward becoming
America's Next Top Model.
—*America's Next Top Model*

————•—————

You are not going to Hollywood.
—*American Idol*

You are not the Biggest Loser.
—*The Biggest Loser*

———•———

You're fired! —*The Apprentice*

———•———

That was your last cut. —*Shear Genius*

———•———

In fashion, you're either in or you're
out. You're out. —*Project Runway*

———•———

You are abolished.
—*America's Most Smartest Model*

———•———

You are the weakest link—goodbye.
—*The Weakest Link*

———•———

Your shot at love has ended.
—*A Shot at Love with Tila Tequila*

———•———

Ladies, those of you who did not receive
a necklace, please leave the chateau.
—*Joe Millionaire*

You're not on the list.
—*I Want to Be a Hilton*

———•••———

You're out of style. —*The Cut*

———•••———

See you later, decorator. —*Top Design*

———•••———

I'm afraid you just don't fit in.
—*The Apprentice: Martha Stewart*

## Shear Genius

Coming up with an exit line for a reality television competition show is no small feat. It needs to be catchy, not too cheesy, and unique to the show. Bravo's *Shear Genius* called upon its viewers to suggest the parting line for departing hairstyling contestants. Here are a few of the best and worst: "Good luck with your next blow job." • "Put a hat on." • "You don't seem to gel." • "Make like your ends, and split."

# ROMANCE IS DEAD

*When love is not forever*

**ROMANCE GIVES US THE HIGHEST** highs—and the lowest lows. Songs proclaim "Your body is a wonderland," then they say simply "Love hurts." Except in those rare instances that love truly is until death do us part, someone's going to have to end things—whether amicably or not. Studies show that doing the breaking up is as stressful as being dumped,

# Tip: Rejecting the Digits

Rather than handling pickup refusals face-to-face or giving out your real contact information, hand out an automated rejection phone number. The caller will hear this recorded message: "Unfortunately, the person who gave you this number does not want to speak to you again. We would like to take this opportunity to officially reject you." Conveniently offered in multiple area codes, the numbers are listed on www.rejectionline.com.

in part because it's so challenging to say the right thing.

Romantic breakups and rejections can occur at many different stages of a relationship—or, in the case of dismissing a pickup attempt, in the complete absence of a relationship. Whether you need to inform a stranger, a one- or two-date wonder, a boyfriend or girlfriend, an aspirant asking marriage on bended knee, or a longtime spouse that the magic is gone, in this chapter you'll find the scripts you need.

Rejecting or breaking up with someone may not be easy, but if it's not working out, it's not worth your time or theirs. When you feel the inevitable pang of guilt, remember that even the most despicable, boring, or repellent individuals deserve to find partners who will love them deeply; by rejecting or breaking up with them, you provide that opportunity. After thusly dismissing their pain, you can move on and find someone better for yourself.

# Putting Down the Pickup

Has that line *ever* worked?

———•———

I liked your approach. Now
let's see your departure.

———•———

Sorry—I don't date outside my species.

———•———

Yes, I come here often. But I
don't think I will anymore.

———•———

I'd like to help you out—which
way did you come in?

———•———

Didn't you hit on me last night?

———•———

I don't have a phone.

———•———

Do I have to spell it out for you?
N-O.

I'm not here to meet anyone.

───•─•───

Even though it doesn't matter to
you that I'm married, it actually
means something to me.

───•─•───

I was winking at someone else.

───•─•───

I know you want to get into
my pants, but there's already
one asshole in there.

───•─•───

Don't make me get out my pepper spray.

## Dumping the Date

You're nice—*too* nice.

───•─•───

Dating would ruin our friendship.

───•─•───

I would eat you alive.

Sorry, I don't date people who like me.

———•—•———

I'd only be going out with you
to make my ex jealous.

———•—•———

You're geographically or
otherwise undesirable.

———•—•———

No need to go any further—
I googled you.

———•—•———

There's a slim possibility
that we're related.

———•—•———

Dogs are great judges of character,
and mine doesn't like you.

———•—•———

We're not astrologically compatible.

———•—•———

I'm really busy for the next few years.

Unfortunately, I just booked my
appointment for revirginization.

———•◆•———

My beer goggles fell off.

———•◆•———

What could possibly have made you
think I would go out with you?

———•◆•———

Aren't you gay?

# Pre-Rejections

In some cases, others are rejecting potential
matches before you even get there. Online
dating site eHarmony denies 20 percent of
its applicants. At the end of an extensive
survey, you're either welcomed into a pool of
tens of millions or you receive this response:
"Participants [must] fall within certain defined
profiles . . . We regret our inability to provide
service for you." Fortunately, you still get your
free Personality Profile.

# Breaking Up: My Fault

I've grown too far beyond you.

———•———

It's not fair to you for me to stay.

———•———

My therapist told me we should break up.

———•———

It's funny—I don't even
want to be friends.

———•———

I need to discover who I am without you.

———•———

For whatever reason,
I can't orgasm with you.

———•———

I think I might be gay.

———•———

I think I might be straight.

———•———

You're way out of my league.

My career is more important
to me than you are.

———•—•———

I love you but I'm not in love with you.

———•—•———

I woke up beside you and
knew it was wrong.

———•—•———

Now that I'm medicated, I realize
that I don't need you anymore.

———•—•———

I'll never convert for you.

———•—•———

I can't forgive myself for cheating.

———•—•———

I'm in love with somebody else.

———•—•———

I'm having some sort of allergic reaction.

———•—•———

I want more sex.
With more people.

# You Need This Chapter

When you try to open your heart to love, chances are you'll lose. One-third of us have been through a breakup in the past ten years. Half of first marriages and 60 percent of remarriages move on to divorce court. But there's still reason for optimism—since singles decide quickly (men, fifteen minutes; women, one hour) if someone is worth a second date, you can use the lines in this chapter to speed up your turnover rate.

I don't want a break. I want a breakup.

I'm just not that into you.

I'm not sure I ever loved you.

If we could just have meaningless sex, I'd be on board.

It's not you, it's me.

## Breaking Up: Your Fault

You're more in love with me
than I am with you.

———•◆•———

I just give and give, and what
do I get? Nothing!

———•◆•———

My mother says I deserve
much better than you.

———•◆•———

You simply don't rock my world.

———•◆•———

Sorry, you're just not "the one."

———•◆•———

It was fun when you were still drinking.

———•◆•———

You're terrible in bed.

———•◆•———

So many things that were cute in the
beginning now get on my nerves.

You're not the same person
I fell in love with.

---

I hate your family.

---

I hate your friends.

---

I hate you.

---

You're a lying, cheating snake.
For some reason, that bothers me.

---

Even after all this time, the hair on
your back really grosses me out.

---

You were thin when we met.

---

You remind me of my
opposite-sex parent.

---

It's not me, it's you.

## Rejecting the Proposal

No thanks.

———•——•———

I'm happy with things the way they are.

———•——•———

That's *such* a huge commitment.

———•——•———

Don't you think it's a little soon?

———•——•———

But I'm not pregnant!

———•——•———

What difference would a
piece of paper make?

———•——•———

Why fix what ain't broken?

———•——•———

You do realize that nearly half of all
marriages end in divorce, right?

———•——•———

Our children will be ugly.

I don't believe in the
institution of marriage.

———•◦•———

It's not legal in this country.

———•◦•———

I've been meaning to tell you that
I think we should end things.

———•◦•———

Your parents hate me. They're always
going to hate me, and they'll
eventually turn you against me.
We don't have a chance in hell.

———•◦•———

I don't see us growing old together.

———•◦•———

I remain traumatized by
my parents' divorce.

———•◦•———

You don't fit my spiritual requirements.

———•◦•———

You're not marriage material.

When I think of us, the word "forever"
just doesn't spring to mind.

———•·•———

What a surprise! If you really knew
me, you'd know that I hate surprises.

———•·•———

Is this a joke?

———•·•———

You call that a ring?

# Tip: The Modern Breakup

Because technology has made so many things
easier, it's tempting to utilize it to deliver bad
romantic news. Text messaging and IM-ing
are best reserved only for the most casual of
rejections. Email and voicemail avoid confrontation but could create fury on the other end.
For any relationship of longer than a month,
face-to-face is the only appropriate means.
And the Post-it as a breakup vessel? Never
recommended.

# Ending the Marriage

Let's end this before death does us part.

———•———

We got married for all the right
reasons, but we're staying together
for all the wrong ones.

———•———

The kids are the ones who suggested it!

———•———

Marriage just isn't as
fun as the wedding.

———•———

Nothing is unconditional.

———•———

I've come to know you better
than anyone, and I've realized
I don't actually like you.

———•———

There are three of us in this
marriage—you, me, and your job.

I've been faking it
since the honeymoon.

———•·•———

I'm suffocating,
and not in a good way.

———•·•———

You're not aging as well as I am.

———•·•———

When we got married,
you were thin.

———•·•———

I can't live with a morning person.

———•·•———

I don't want to waste any
more of my life on you.

———•·•———

It's time for me to upgrade.

———•·•———

The party's over.

# LOVED ONES
# BE GONE

*When others are bringing you down*

A TIME-WORN ADAGE STATES,
"You can pick your friends, and
you can pick your nose, but you
can't pick your family." While
on one level that's true, we are
no longer obligated to put up
with family members who bring
us down, and we sometimes find
ourselves with friends who no
longer add value to our lives.
In contemporary times, friends

# Tip: Kick the Kids Out

Nearly four million adults between the ages of twenty-five and thirty-four still live with their parents after returning from college or a failed marriage—or never having left at all. For these "boomerang kids," the family home staves off financial responsibility and other pesky aspects of maturity. These parents should recognize that not only have they done their eighteen-year job, they're doing their kids a major life-lesson disservice. Get them out of there!

can be family, and family can be friends—and both can be foes, making for simultaneous indispensability and dispos-ability. Finally, pets are now family members and BFFs, and as such it's sometimes necessary to reject them in the moment or give them the ultimate heave-ho.

When the time comes to reject or break up with family members, their hold can be so deep and strong that it's difficult to find just the right words. Breaking up with lovers can be easier than breaking up with friends because there's a longstanding tradition of such interactions. Because pets don't talk, we don't plan out the speeches essential to make the breach. In this chapter, you'll find lines to script all these challenging encounters.

People and pets come into your life for a reason, a season, or a lifetime. Once you've decided that "lifetime" is not to be, it's better to rid yourself of the bad seeds than continue subjecting yourself to unnecessary obligations.

# Child to Parent

I blame you for everything!

---

It'll all be clear when you
read my memoir.

---

You never loved me.

---

When I look at you,
I hope I was adopted!

---

I have my own values now,
and I don't value you.

---

I should have emancipated myself
before I turned eighteen.

---

I have my own family now, and
it doesn't include you.

You're right—you were a terrible parent.

---

I raised myself!

## Parent to Child

You were a mistake.

---

I'm not your real daddy.

---

We were hoping you wouldn't come back.

---

I could have been so much
more without you.

---

You're such a disappointment.

---

I thought we got rid of you after college!

---

You steal all of the attention.

We've converted your room
into our personal gym.

---

Really, you've done enough.

---

I disown you.

---

You're dead to me.

## Sibling to Sibling

You must be adopted.

---

They should have
left you at the hospital.

---

I have always been the favorite.

---

Now that I'm out from under your
shadow, I refuse to live in the dark!

I can't talk to you until you've
been adequately diagnosed.

———•◦•———

We have nothing in common other
than sharing the same parents.

———•◦•———

Now that I have friends,
I don't need you anymore.

———•◦•———

You're more trouble than you're worth.

# Family Turmoil

Most guilt derives from negative feelings
toward family members. Fortunately, you're
not alone: "Happy families are all alike; every
unhappy family is unhappy in its own way."
—Leo Tolstoy • "Relations are simply a tedious
pack of people, who haven't got the remot-
est knowledge of how to live, nor the smallest
instinct about when to die." —Oscar Wilde •
"All people are your relatives, therefore expect
only trouble from them." —Chinese proverb

My children have plenty of aunts
and uncles to choose from.

## Extended Family to Extended Family

You're only my third cousin.

———•—•———

You're more like an acquaintance
than a relative.

———•—•———

Blood is overrated.

———•—•———

I don't have to have a relationship with
you just because you're on my family tree.

———•—•———

You're crazy—everyone says so.

———•—•———

I'm not giving you any more money, and
I never want to hear from you again.

———•—•———

I don't even believe that we're related.

## Friend to Friend

You're more like an
acquaintance than a friend.

———•••———

I'm not in a position to be a
friend to anyone right now.

———•••———

You're never there for me when
I need you, so I figure, why
bother when I don't need you?

———•••———

It's not worth getting to know you.

———•••———

I already have enough friends.

———•••———

I regret to tell you that
I have to phase you out.

———•••———

You're a total user.

# Networking Rejection

On social networking sites such as MySpace and Facebook, the definition of "friend" is rather loose; sometimes it's necessary to clean house. Fortunately, in cyberland, it's easy to delete people from your list and your life—or curtail unwanted connections from the get-go and reject their invitations. This works for IM-ing as well. If you delete someone from your buddy list, they'll probably get the hint.

You're a total loser.

You don't mesh well with the group.

I'm trying to stay positive right now, and your energy is totally negative.

You party too much.

You're no fun.

---

Everything's about you.

---

Now that I'm married,
I don't need friends.

---

Now that I have kids, I'm only
friends with other people
who have children.

---

We don't have any friendship chemistry.

---

I don't have time for your
drama anymore.

---

You were thin when we met.

---

I took you on as a pity case; now
you seem to be doing better.

Friends don't let friends befriend you.

———◆◆◆———

We've been through so much together,
and I don't want to go through any more.

———◆◆◆———

You drain my soul.

———◆◆◆———

You know too much.

———◆◆◆———

I've evolved, you haven't.

———◆◆◆———

I hate you, and I'm not the only one.

———◆◆◆———

I want to forgive you, and
I want to *forget* you.

## Human to Pet

Down!

———◆◆◆———

Get off me!

Stay there.

———•—•———

Stop licking me!

———•—•———

Stop humping me!

———•—•———

The gate was left open for a reason.

———•—•———

We decided the pet door
was too unsightly.

———•—•———

You shed too much.

———•—•———

You don't match my new couch.

———•—•———

You no longer fit in my purse.

———•—•———

All you do is swim in circles.

———•—•———

The neighbors want you more.

Now that we've had kids, we
have no more need for you.

———•———

We were told that you could talk.

———•———

All you do is meow.

———•———

The food, the toys, the vet, the
grooming, the dry cleaning
bills—you're just not worth it!

———•———

I've suddenly gone allergic.

———•———

It turns out ferrets are
illegal in this state.

———•———

You really don't seem to
have your own life.

———•———

You'll never be anything but a loser.

You steal all of the attention.

—◆—

You have dog breath.

—◆—

I have a new best friend.

—◆—

I just know you'll love the pound.

—◆—

Off!

# Tip: Losing Your Pet

Cats and dogs are by far the most popular
pets, but fortunately they can make for the
easiest nonhuman breakups. Sending them
off into the world ill-equipped can be the best
way to rid yourself of an unwanted nuisance.
Make sure you don't microchip them, outfit
them with identifying collar and tags, or put
up signs announcing their absence. The good
news? Nearly 90 percent of "lost" pets—
those without ID—are never found.

*"You were cute when you were little,
but now you're just a menace."*